Full Speed Ahead

The Science of Going Fast

Library of Congress Cataloging-in-Publication Data

Schuh, Mari C.
  Full speed ahead : the science of going fast / by Mari C. Schuh.
    p. cm. -- (Shockwave)
  Includes index.

ISBN-10: 0-531-17792-0 (lib. bdg.)
ISBN-13: 978-0-531-17792-1 (lib. bdg.)
ISBN-10: 0-531-18835-3 (pbk.)
ISBN-13: 978-0-531-18835-4 (pbk.)

1. Speed--Juvenile literature. 2. Acceleration (Mechanics)--Juvenile literature.
I. Title. II. Series.

  QC137.52.S34 2008
  531'.11--dc22

2007012226

Published in 2008 by Children's Press, an imprint of Scholastic Inc.,
557 Broadway, New York, New York 10012
www.scholastic.com

SCHOLASTIC, CHILDREN'S PRESS, and associated logos are trademarks
and/or registered trademarks of Scholastic Inc.

08 09 10 11 12 13 14 15 16 17
10 9 8 7 6 5 4 3 2 1

Printed in China through Colorcraft Ltd., Hong Kong

Author: Mari C. Schuh
Educational Consultant: Ian Morrison
Editor: Lynette Evans
Designer: Emma Alsweiler
Photo Researcher: Jamshed Mistry

Photographs by: Getty Images (runners, p. 11; p. 21); **Jennifer and Brian Lupton**
(girl, p. 32); **NASA/Dryden Flight Research Center** (p. 25, p. 34); **NASA/Marshall Space
Flight Center** (p. 26); **Photodisc** (p. 27); **Photolibrary** (p. 3; taxi, p. 11; p. 12; hovercraft,
p. 13; p. 15; Saleen S-7R twin turbo car, p. 17; p. 18; p. 29); **Tranz: Corbis** (cover;
pp. 7–10; hydroplane, p. 13; p. 14; p. 16; Melanie Troxel, NHRA racing, p. 17;
pp. 19–20; pp. 22–24; pp. 30–31; rush-hour traffic, pp. 32–33); **Rex Features** (p. 28)

All illustrations and other photographs © Weldon Owen Education Inc.

Full Speed Ahead

The Science of Going Fast

Mari C. Schuh

children's press®

An imprint of Scholastic Inc.

NEW YORK • TORONTO • LONDON • AUCKLAND • SYDNEY
MEXICO CITY • NEW DELHI • HONG KONG
DANBURY, CONNECTICUT

CHECK THESE OUT!

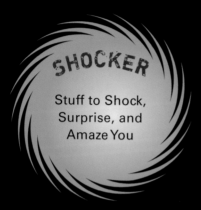

SHOCKER
Stuff to Shock,
Surprise, and
Amaze You

Quick Recaps
and Notable
Notes

Word Stunners
and Other Oddities

The Heads-Up
on Expert Reading

Links to More
Information

CONTENTS

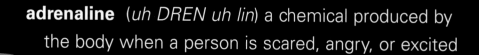

adrenaline (*uh DREN uh lin*) a chemical produced by the body when a person is scared, angry, or excited

aerodynamic (*air oh dye NAM mik*) shaped to move through the air easily and quickly

air resistance the slowing down of an object as it pushes against the air

atmosphere (*AT muss feer*) the layer of gases surrounding the earth

friction a force that slows down an object whenever it touches something else, such as another surface

gravity the force that pulls objects toward the earth

momentum (*moh MEN tum*) the force produced by a moving object. This depends on the object's speed and mass.

For additional vocabulary, see Glossary on page 34.

Nouns ending in *um* sometimes form plurals by dropping the *um* and adding *a*. So the plural of *momentum* is *momenta*. Other examples include *stadium/stadia*; *aquarium/aquaria*; *maximum/maxima*. Now it is becoming more acceptable in many cases to just add *s*.

A roller coaster gathers **momentum** as it races down a steep track.

Speed is a measure of how quickly things move.
People like to be able to travel at high speeds.
They have invented machines that help them go fast.
The technology used in boats, cars, trains, and planes
has improved greatly over the years. People have
learned what forces slow machines down. They have
found ways to make machines travel faster.

Some machines today can reach very high speeds.
These machines are especially built for speed.
They are sleek and lightweight. People who ride
in these fast machines are strapped in for safety.
They wear safety gear, such as helmets
and face masks. Sometimes they wear
fireproof suits and gloves too.

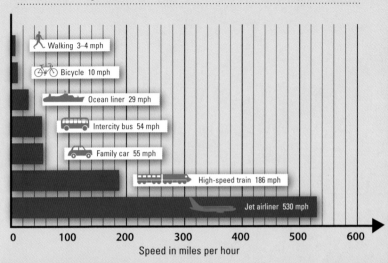

Common Speeds of Some Kinds of Transportation

Walking 3–4 mph
Bicycle 10 mph
Ocean liner 29 mph
Intercity bus 54 mph
Family car 55 mph
High-speed train 186 mph
Jet airliner 530 mph

| 0 | 100 | 200 | 300 | 400 | 500 | 600 |

Speed in miles per hour

Some inventions haven't taken off.
Others have been a roaring success!

The Need for Speed

Most people are used to high-speed travel today. Cars, buses, and fast trains zoom along roads or rails built for maximum speed. Powerful ships carry passengers over the seas. Sleek jets crisscross the skies. Many of today's fast machines are used for transportation. Others are used for the thrill of going fast.

> After reading the first sentence, I am fairly certain of what the rest of the paragraph will be about. This makes reading easier.

Some people can travel at high speeds, even without machines. For most people, however, technology has increased their pace. Before fast machines, people walked or ran. Sometimes they used horses, donkeys, or camels to take them places. These animals are still used in parts of the world today. However, they are far from speedy.

What Is Speed?

Moving objects are all around us. Speed is a term used to describe the distance an object travels in a certain amount of time. For example, if a car moves at a speed of 40 feet per second, it will travel a distance of 80 feet in two seconds.

Racing on Water

People from Egypt may have been the first to use boats to move goods. They used large wooden oars to row boats down the Nile River about five thousand years ago. Then they added sails. Sails trapped the wind. The boats could travel even faster.

People still use sails to capture the power of the wind. However, modern technology lets us travel across water even faster. Racing boats use gasoline, diesel, jet, or **turbine** engines. Propellers help a boat go faster. They help keep it on course. Hydroplanes are among the fastest racing boats. They travel on a cushion of air. Only a small part of a hydroplane touches the water as it skims across. There is almost no **friction** to slow it down.

In the word *hydroplane*, *hydro* means "water." Other words beginning with *hydro* include: *hydroelectric*, *hydrogen*, and *hydrophobia*.

Hydroplanes skim across the water in almost the same way a flat stone does when skipped.

Hovercraft

Know the Science

What Is Friction?

Friction is a force that makes objects resist moving past one another. It slows them down. Hydroplanes and other air cushion vehicles, such as hovercraft, have a layer of air between the surface of the boat and the surface of the water. This gets rid of much of the friction. It helps them travel fast.

Talk About Trains

Trains were invented in the early 1800s. They made a great difference in the speed at which people could travel. The first trains were not fast by today's standards. But by 1964, the "bullet train" was speeding through Japan. At first, it traveled up to 131 miles per hour. Today, bullet trains can reach speeds of 188 miles per hour.

First train to enter Washington D.C., 1835

Maglev trains are fast, supersmooth trains. Maglev trains don't have wheels. They use **magnetic force** instead. Powerful magnets enable the trains to float just above the tracks. The trains do not touch the tracks. Computers turn **electromagnets** in the tracks on and off as needed. Maglev trains can zoom along at speeds of up to 300 miles per hour.

The word *maglev* is a contraction. It is made up of the words *magnetic* and *levitation*.

Maglev train

What Is Magnetic Force?

A magnet is a metal that attracts iron and some other materials. Around a magnet is an area called the magnetic field. This is the area in which a magnet has a force. If another magnet comes into this magnetic field, it will either be attracted to the magnet or repel the magnet. Magnets on maglev trains push away magnets in the track. This allows the train to rise above the track. It reduces friction. This lets the train travel quickly and smoothly.

Freight train

Trains can travel fast, but they can't stop quickly. Some freight trains are so long and so heavy that they need a mile to stop. That's the length of about 18 football fields!

Burning Rubber

In 1908, Henry Ford made a car that was cheap enough for most people to buy. His Model T car could reach a top speed of 45 miles per hour. Drivers had trouble getting up long, steep hills in a Model T. This was because the fuel tank was mounted beneath the driver's seat. It was behind the engine. The fuel didn't always flow well to the engine. To solve this, drivers would drive the car up a hill backwards!

Cars have changed a lot since the early days. Some cars are now made for high speed. Most fast cars have a sleek, **aerodynamic** shape. The Saleen S-7 twin turbo car is one of the fastest luxury cars in the world today. It can reach speeds of 250 miles per hour. It goes from 0 to 60 miles per hour in just three seconds.

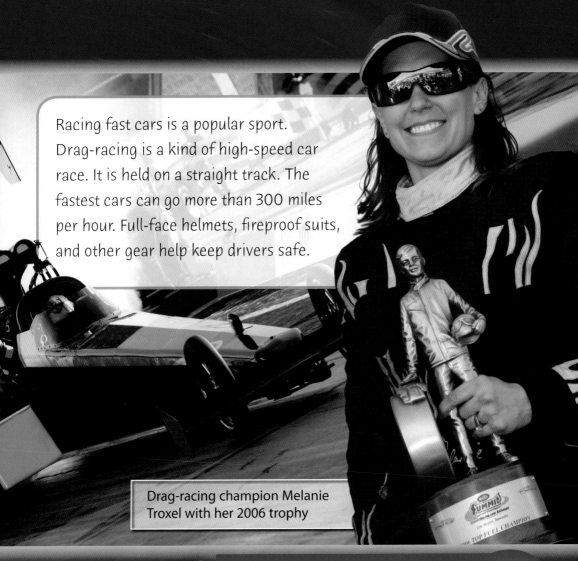

Racing fast cars is a popular sport. Drag-racing is a kind of high-speed car race. It is held on a straight track. The fastest cars can go more than 300 miles per hour. Full-face helmets, fireproof suits, and other gear help keep drivers safe.

Drag-racing champion Melanie Troxel with her 2006 trophy

Saleen S-7R

What Are Aerodynamics?

The movement of objects is slowed by **molecules** in the air. This is known as **air resistance**. The faster an object moves, the more air resistance it meets. Most modern planes, trains, boats, and cars have a shape that allows air to flow easily around them. This is called an aerodynamic shape. These vehicles can travel at high speeds more safely. This is because they are not being **buffeted** by air currents.

17

Stock cars go around wide oval tracks. Stock-car racing is the most popular kind of automobile racing in the United States. Races go on for many hours. Wide tracks let cars pass each other for a chance to win. During races, stock cars surge to speeds of 150 to 200 miles per hour. No wonder so many people love to watch these races!

•••••• **Did You Know?** ••••••••▶

During races, drivers pull into special areas called pits for refueling and repairs. During pit stops, skilled crews change tires in just seconds. Workers think about every detail on these super-speedy cars. Small adjustments can make a big difference when it comes to speed.

Go-cart race

Stock-car race

Many top race-car drivers first learn to drive with go-carts. Go-carts are fast little cars. They can race around tracks at very high speeds. Go-carts can dash by at more than 100 miles per hour. Helmets and safety belts are a must!

Speed Machines

You might not recognize an early motorcycle if you saw one. At first, motorcycles weren't much more than bicycles with motors strapped on! They were made of wood. They didn't go very fast.

Today, motorcycles are speed machines. Many race around tracks at incredible speeds. Drivers make use of **centripetal force** to speed around curves. They go so fast that the bikes appear as just one big blur. Many motorcycles can now reach speeds of 200 miles per hour. The MTT Turbine Superbike can travel even faster. This speed machine has raced at more than 220 miles per hour.

Motorcycles	
Early	Modern
• wooden	• metal
• quite slow	• very fast
• uncomfortable	• comfortable
• clunky	• aerodynamic

SHOCKER

Billy Baxter holds the Blindfold Motorcycle Speed Record. In 2003, he put on a blindfold and set off. He cruised at 165 miles per hour on his motorcycle!

Know the Science

What Is Centripetal Force?

Centripetal force is a force that causes an object to move in a curved, or circular path. Without forces, all objects would move in a straight line at a constant speed. When a motorbike speeds around a curve, the friction between the tires and the ground creates centripetal force. This force helps to keep the bike moving in a curve.

Faster Than Sound

Airplane designs have changed hugely since the Wright brothers first took to the skies over Kitty Hawk in 1903. The Wright brothers reached a speed of 30 miles per hour. During World War I (1914–1918), fighter pilots battled in the skies. Later, stunt pilots made their planes perform at air shows and races. The fastest reached speeds of up to 253 miles per hour!

In 1947, a pilot named Chuck Yeager made history. He traveled faster than the **speed of sound**. He flew his jet up to 700 miles per hour. He broke through the sound barrier. During these early days of high-speed flying, experts studied the effects of speed on the human body.

What Is the Speed of Sound?

At sea level, sound travels in air at an average speed of 761 miles per hour. Jet airplanes sometimes fly faster than the speed of sound. They travel at **supersonic** speeds.

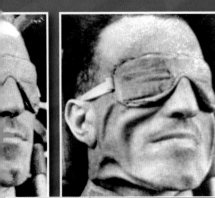

A test pilot withstands the effects of traveling at 275 to 350 miles per hour.

Today, strong jet engines provide the power for airplanes to reach high speeds. The Boeing 747 is the world's fastest **subsonic** jetliner. It cruises the skies at 567 miles per hour. The 747 lands back on the ground at 160 miles per hour. This speedy machine is not only fast, it is also huge. The 747 can hold more than 400 people. No wonder people call it a jumbo jet!

Boeing 747
- fastest subsonic jetliner
- flies at 567 mph
- lands at 160 mph
- carries more than 400 people per flight

The fastest airplane in the world today is the Lockheed SR-71 Blackbird. It travels at speeds of around 2,200 miles per hour. In 1974, the SR-71 flew from New York to London in less than two hours! Most commercial jets take about seven hours to fly from New York to London. They could travel faster, but aircraft traveling at higher speeds use more fuel.

Boeing assembly plant

Lockheed SR-71 Blackbird

SHOCKER

The wing of a 747 jet measures 5,600 square feet. That is big enough to hold 45 medium-sized automobiles!

• • • • • **Did You Know?**

A jumbo jet has six million parts! Half of the parts are fasteners. These keep everything in place. Every one of its parts helps make the jumbo jet the fastest and safest aircraft that it can be.

Blasting Off!

3, 2, 1, liftoff! The space shuttle overcomes **gravity** and blasts into the sky. But how does it get its power? The answer is fuel, fuel, and even more fuel. Rocket boosters on the shuttle hold more than two million pounds of solid fuel! The shuttle also has a tank that carries more than a half million gallons of gas.

Why all the fuel, you ask? A space shuttle must escape the powerful force of the earth's gravity. To do this, it must reach a speed of about 17,500 miles per hour. That's about five miles per second! The space shuttle keeps building speed until it reaches orbit in space. To get out of the earth's orbit, the shuttle needs to reach a speed of 24,000 miles per hour.

On this page, the author seems to be asking me questions, and then giving me the answers. This is an interesting way of getting my attention. It sure works for me.

Fuel tank being transported to a launch site

Fuel tank

What Is Gravity?

Gravity is the force that gives everything on the earth its weight. It is the force that pulls things toward the ground. Overcoming gravity is the biggest challenge for a space mission. A powerful rocket called a launch vehicle, or booster, helps a spacecraft overcome gravity.

SHOCKER

In 2001, American Dennis Tito became the world's first space tourist. He paid $20 million for his ticket. He took a high-speed ride into space on a Russian spacecraft. It docked at the International Space Station.

Did You Know?

The external fuel tank is the largest single piece of a space shuttle. The giant cylinder is higher than a 15-story building. It holds 526,000 gallons of **propellant**. This is all burned during the first few minutes of flight.

Zoom Into the Future

One day, we could all be zipping through the sky on a daily basis. Have you heard of skycars? They seem like cartoon vehicles. However, experts believe that skycars could be a practical means of transportation in the future. A "highway in the sky" could help reduce crowded roads. People would no longer have to wait in traffic. Scientists are developing skycar technology to make skycars safe and easy to use.

There's no doubt that, even today, planes fly fast. In the future, however, they could fly even faster. NASA is working to create a practical supersonic jet called a **scramjet**. Pilots are carrying out test flights. Scramjets are made to dart across the sky in a very short time. High-tech engines would enable the jets to fly 15 times faster than the speed of sound.

An example of how a skycar might look as it flies over a city

An artist's impression of a scramjet

How Does a Scramjet Work?

Scramjets are designed to be smaller, lighter, and faster than other jets. This is because the oxygen the engines need in order to fire is to be taken from the **atmosphere** passing through the vehicle instead of from large, heavy oxygen tanks onboard. Rockets combine a liquid fuel with liquid oxygen to blast off. By taking away the need for liquid oxygen onboard, an aircraft can be smaller and faster.

It's Such a Rush

Why do people like to go so fast? Speed gives us a rush of excitement. Sometimes we are even a little bit frightened. Our bodies make more of a chemical called **adrenaline** when we go fast. Adrenaline can make our bodies stronger. It causes our hearts to beat faster. Our blood flows faster. We even breathe faster.

Many people love driving fast cars and motorcycles. Some people claim that speed gives them energy. The rush of adrenaline makes them feel more alert. But the thrill of speed can come at a high price. Speeding along a road is very dangerous behavior. It's better to leave speed to the professionals!

SHOCKER

Watch out for speeding furniture! In 1998, Edd China and David Davenport wanted to have a new kind of adrenaline rush. Their motorized sofa is the fastest furniture in the world. It reached a top speed of 87 miles per hour. That's faster than some cars on the highway!

Amusement parks are popular destinations for people who like to get an adrenaline rush! Roller coasters gather **momentum** as they speed down a track. They provide a fast ride.

What Is Adrenaline?

Adrenaline is a hormone produced by the adrenal glands. It is also called epinephrine. When a person becomes angry or frightened, the adrenal glands release large amounts of adrenaline into the bloodstream. This hormone helps the body cope with sudden stress. It causes changes in the body to prepare it to fight or flee.

Many people have become used to living in a fast-paced, high-speed society. We eat fast foods. We expect instant communication over the Internet. Regular mail seems so slow, we often call it snail mail. We become impatient when traffic is reduced to a crawl during "rush hour." We want faster travel and a faster lifestyle. But is faster always better?

WHAT DO YOU THINK?

Should people keep on creating faster machines for faster travel?

PRO

I think it is good that people try to go faster. This will mean that we waste much less time. We can also reach people who need help quickly. Fast machines are exciting to ride in. They can also be good examples of art, design, and technology.

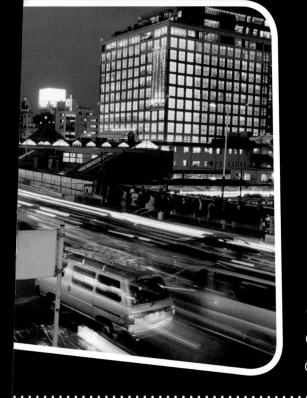

The faster we travel, the more fuel we use. The **fossil fuels** that most vehicles use are **nonrenewable**. They need to be conserved. Also, the faster we travel, the harder we can crash. Many people are killed in high-speed crashes every day. And although an adrenaline buzz can be energizing, continual rushing around can put stresses and strains on the body.

CON

It is terrible to use up the earth's valuable fuel supplies just to go faster. People could live healthier, happier lives if they weren't always rushing to get places. I would rather take the time to enjoy what's around me as I travel somewhere.

GLOSSARY

buffet (*BUH fit*) to strike repeatedly, as waves against a shore

centripetal (*sen TRIP uh tuhl*) **force** the force that keeps an object moving in a curve

electromagnet a piece of iron that becomes a magnet when an electric current flows around it

fossil fuel a fuel, such as coal, oil, or natural gas, that was formed in the ground from plant or animal remains

magnetic force the attractive or repulsive force experienced by iron and some other materials when near a magnet

molecule (*MOL uh kyool*) the smallest particle into which a substance can be divided while still being part of the same substance

nonrenewable resources that are not able to be replaced after having been used

propellant a high-performance fuel used by a rocket engine

scramjet a supersonic jet that is being developed and will travel fifteen times faster than the speed of sound

speed of sound the speed that a sound wave travels. The speed of sound in air at sea level is 761 mph.

subsonic moving slower than the speed of sound

supersonic moving faster than the speed of sound

turbine (*TUR bine*) an engine driven by water, steam, or gas passing through the blades of a wheel and making it turn

Scramjet

FIND OUT MORE

BOOKS

Beyer, Mark. *Transportation of the Future*. Children's Press, 2002.

Cefrey, Holly. *High Speed Trains*. Children's Press, 2001.

Herbst, Judith. *The History of Transportation*. Twenty-First Century Books, 2006.

Morris, Neil. *Mega Book of Aircraft*. Smart Apple Media, 2003.

Parham, Jerrill. *Thrills and Spills: Fast Sport*s. Scholastic Inc., 2008.

Schaefer, Adam R. *Roller Coasters*. Capstone Press, 2005.

Stevens, Ian. *Extreme Machines*. Bearport Publishing, 2006.

WEB SITES

Go to the Web sites below
to learn more about
transportation.

www.americanhistory.si.edu/onthemove

www.trakkies.co.uk/history/history.htm

www.nasa.gov/missions/research/f_scramjets.html

www.worldalmanacforkids.com/explore/sports/autoracing.html

INDEX

ABOUT THE AUTHOR

Mari C. Schuh writes nonfiction books for kids of all ages. She writes about all kinds of things, including volcanoes, termites, zombies, and transportation. In the summer, she enjoys zooming across lakes on boats with her friends. Mari likes to board high-tech trains for shopping and sight-seeing trips. Her favorite part about flying on planes is the loud, powerful takeoff. Mari used to ride roller coasters, but now she finds them way too fast!